Careers

371.425

TECHNOLOGY AT WORK

ON THE

FILM SET

Richard Spilsbury

www.raintreepublishers.co.uk
Visit our website to find out more information about Raintree books.

To order:
☎ Phone 44 (0) 1865 888112
🖹 Send a fax to 44 (0) 1865 314091
💻 Visit the Raintree bookshop at www.raintreepublishers.co.uk to browse our catalogue and order online.

Raintree is an imprint of Pearson Education Limited, a company incorporated in England and Wales having its registered office at Edinburgh Gate, Harlow, Essex, CM20 2JE – Registered company number: 00872828

Raintree is a registered trademark of Pearson Education Ltd.

Edited by Louise Galpine and Rachel Howells
Designed by Richard Parker and Tinstar Design Ltd
Original illustrations© by Pearson Education Ltd
Illustrations by Darren Lingard
Picture Research by Hannah Taylor and Catherine Bevan
Originated by Modern Age
Printed and bound in China by CTPS

13-digit ISBN 978 1 4062 0984 6
13 12 11 10 09
10 9 8 7 6 5 4 3 2 1

British Library Cataloguing in Publication Data
Spilsbury, Richard,
   On the film set. - (Technology at work)
   778.5'3
A full catalogue record for this book is available from the British Library.

Acknowledgements
The publishers would like to thank the following for permission to reproduce photographs: ©Alamy (Seapix) p. **7**; ©The Kobal Collection pp. **11** (Studio Canal/ Working Title), **13** (Joseph Lederer/ Wayans Bros/ Revolution Studios), **17** (Universal/ Wing Nut Films) , **20-21** (Castle Rock/ Shangri-La Entertainment), **22** (20th Century Fox); ©Photodisc pp. **5**, **29**; ©Photoedit Inc pp. **14** (David R. Frazier), **23** (Michael Newman); ©Photolibrary (Image Source) p. **27**; ©Rex Features (ITV) p. **15**; ©Ronald Grant Archive pp. **4** (Warner Bros/ Saul Zaentz Co), **12** (Rivdel Films/ Film Features/ Cinemarque Entertainment BV), **18** (Lionsgate Films), **19**.

Cover photograph of a movie camera, reproduced with permission of ©Corbis (Douglas Kirkland).

We would like to thank Ian Graham for his invaluable help in the preparation of this book.

Every effort has been made to contact copyright holders of any material reproduced in this book. Any omissions will be rectified in subsequent printings if notice is given to the publishers.

CONTENTS

Some words are printed in bold, **like this**. You can find out what they mean by looking in the glossary.

THE FILM SET

Have you ever been in a cinema and wondered how and where the film was made? The place a film or movie is made is called a film set. The group of people that make the film are called a **film crew**. The people in the film crew have different jobs. For example, some people record sound, some put make-up on the actors, and others create **special effects**.

On this film set, the crew are using a wind machine to make it look like the actors are in a hurricane storm.

Movie machines

Movies are made using a variety of **machines**. Machines are devices that do work for us. For example, the film crew use movie cameras to record pictures. All machines need **energy** to make them work. Lights need electrical energy to make their bulbs glow.

The film crew bang a clapperboard to mark the start of every separate section of film they make.

AT WORK

WHO'S WHO IN A FILM CREW?

producer	raises money to make a film and hires actors and film crew
director	controls what the film is like and tells the actors and film crew what to do
camera operator	uses cameras to record action on film
gaffer	in charge of lighting the actors and film set
production sound mixer	records sounds during filming

LIGHTS

Shining bright light from a **spotlight** on something is a way of making it stand out. For example, light on an actor's face helps us see their expression. Different kinds of light can create different moods. Dim light creates dark shadows that feel mysterious. Scenes lit with red light look warmer than those lit with blue light.

Folding flaps on spotlights like this control how much light they produce. Spotlights are often supported on strong legs called tripods.

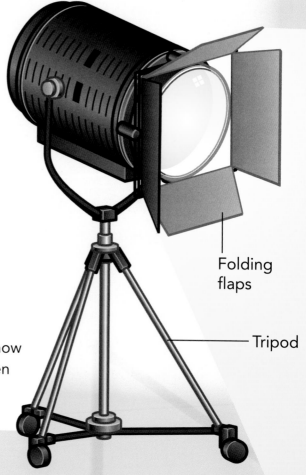

Folding flaps

Tripod

AT WORK

MAKING LIGHT

Bulbs in spotlights work in two main ways. In some bulbs thin coils of wire glow brightly when electricity flows through them. The electrical **energy** turns into light and heat energy because the coils slow down the flow of electricity. Other spotlight bulbs glow when electricity flows through special gases and metals inside tubes.

In the spotlight

Some spotlights shine on the actors as they move around.
There may be lights pointed at their front, side, and back to light
the actors properly. Sometimes the lights are aimed at white
reflective panels. These panels bounce back more gentle light
than a spotlight.

You can change
light colours by
putting **filters**,
or transparent
coloured glass
or plastic screens,
over spotlights.

CAMERA

When the action begins on the film set the camera operator records it using a movie camera. Movie cameras take lots of individual images (pictures) one after the other. When these images flick past very quickly they appear to move.

Screen

2

Light

Lens

1

5

4

K825

K825 ·

3

1. The camera operator looks through the eyepiece to see what images come through the lens.

2. Light from the actors and scenery enters the movie camera.

3. Light strikes a digital **sensor** made up of many small light-sensitive squares. Each square converts light into electricity. The amount of electricity and how fast it flows depends on the brightness and colour of the light.

4. A **computer chip** in the camera converts information from each square into an image.

5. Some images are recorded onto strips of film in movie cameras. Most are stored in the camera's computer memory or recorded onto video tape.

AT WORK

TRICKING THE BRAIN

We are able to see because our brain puts together images from light detected by our eyes. Our brain stores the images briefly. When we see more than 12 images each second, our brain blends together the stored and new images. Differences between the images become smoothed out. Our brain has been tricked into seeing moving pictures!

CHANGING THE VIEW

In a film, the view can switch from a close-up of someone's face to a long-distance view of hills or a crowd of people. This variety of views makes films more interesting to watch. Camera operators change the view by using different **lenses** on the front of the camera. Lenses are made up of several curved glass or plastic pieces that direct light onto the camera's **sensor**.

Wide-angle lenses let in light from a wide area in front of the camera. Telephoto lenses have a narrower view for close-ups.

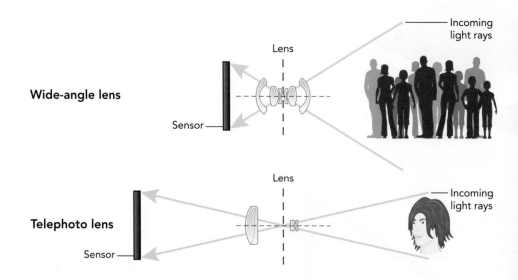

Wide-angle lens

Lens

Incoming light rays

Sensor

Telephoto lens

Lens

Incoming light rays

Sensor

AT WORK

STOPPING SHAKING

If a camera operator shakes a bit, the sensor in a movie camera can move up and down. This makes the images blurred. Many lenses have image stabilization to stop this. A piece in the lens floats in oil and the **computer chip** in the camera uses information about its position to create a shake-free image.

Moving around

Camera operators move around to get the best view of actors or objects in a film studio. They sometimes shift heavy cameras on a wheeled trolley called a dolly. The dolly often runs on tracks. Sometimes operators lift cameras high in the air on long arms called jibs.

Using a camera dolly on a track helps to keep the camera steady when it moves. Then the camera operator can film smoothly with less camera shake.

CHANGING LOOKS

Make-up artists can make actors look heavier or older than they really are. They sometimes put make-up on an actor's face, such as lines around eyes to look like wrinkles. Make-up artists can also transform the shape of an actor's face using latex (rubber) masks. This is how actors can look like aliens, animals, and all kinds of imaginary characters.

The first stage in creating a mask for a particular actor is to cover their face in a special paste.

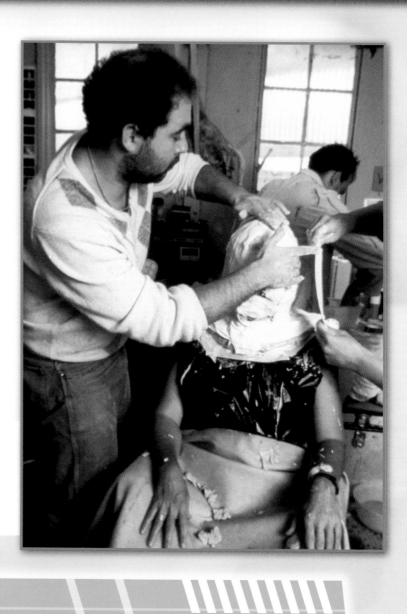

AT WORK

A NEW FACE EVERY DAY?

Latex masks sometimes take hours to put on. They cannot be used twice because they get damaged when actors take them off. So new ones need to be made on each day of filming!

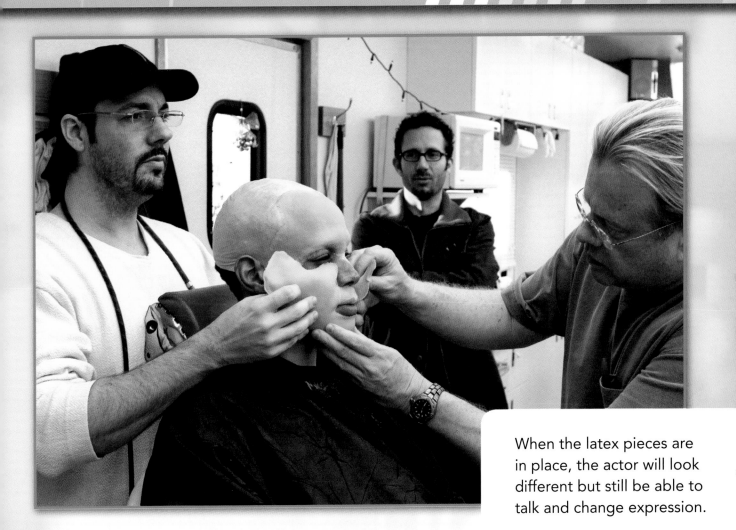

When the latex pieces are in place, the actor will look different but still be able to talk and change expression.

Making a mask

To make a mask, the make-up artist spreads paste called alginate over the actor's face. The alginate sets into a **mould**. The artist removes the mould and pours in wet Plaster of Paris. This sets hard into a life-like **cast** of the actor's face. The artist makes this cast into a new character by sticking on clay pieces. They make a mould of each piece and cast pieces of latex in the moulds. The artist sticks the latex pieces on and blends them with the actor's skin using make-up.

IN THE BACKGROUND

A film is believable if the background or setting looks real. **Film crews** sometimes make films in real places or **locations**, or they can create false backgrounds in a studio. Some imaginary backgrounds, such as a space city, are so difficult to construct that skilled artists draw them using computers.

The film crew uses **machines** such as drills, hammers, and saws to cut and fix together pieces of wood for film backgrounds.

COBWEB SHOOTER!

When a film crew wants to make a background look old or spooky they might reach for a cobweb shooter. This is a special hot glue gun that melts sticks of web glue and sprays it out. The web glue cools as it sprays out into lots of thin strands. These stick on backgrounds and look like old cobwebs.

Constructing sets

In a studio the film crew build some backgrounds from wood, which they paint to look like other materials. On a film set a castle wall may be made of plastic painted to look like real stone. The crew adds objects, or **props**, in the background to make it look real. Props might include anything from potted plants to a sink full of dirty dishes!

The only way you can tell that this is a film set and not a normal bedroom is because of the **spotlights** overhead.

REMOVING COLOURS

Have you ever seen a film with an actor hanging from a ledge on a high building, or perhaps flying above the ground? Special bluescreen technology makes things like this possible in films without putting actors in any danger.

How bluescreen technology works

First, the camera operator films the background without any actors. Then they make a film of actors pretending to do something dangerous against a plain blue (or sometimes green) background. When the two films are put together, the plain background colour is removed so the actor looks like they are really in serious trouble or flying!

The actor is filmed in front of a plain blue background.

A special computer removes the blue from every separate image. This leaves just the actor on each image of the film.

Finally, workers combine this actor film with the background film.

This shot was combined with background animated film to make it look like actress Naomi Watts is being gripped by the mighty hand of King Kong.

AT WORK

BLUE OR GREEN BACKGROUND?

Human skin colours range from pink to dark brown. These colours are very different to green and blue. That is why blue and green are used as background colours. Removing these colours from film of actors does not make the actors' skin look a funny colour.

SPECIAL EFFECTS

Special effects can make it look like spaceships landing on Earth or magical creatures flying above a city are real. Different types of technology create special effects. To show a car blowing up, a **film crew** sets off special explosions. They lift actors and car parts into the air on wires so it looks like they are lifted up by the blast!

The weight of the actor is balanced by a slightly smaller load. This makes it easier for the film crew to lift them up.

AT WORK

SECRET STARS

Next time you see your favourite film stars doing something dangerous, remember it probably is not them. Sometimes an actor's place is taken by someone who looks like the actor. This worker is specially trained not to get hurt when doing dangerous tricks or **stunts**.

Computer effects

Some special effects are computer generated images, or **CGI**. Some films are entirely made up of **three-dimensional** (3D) computer images. In other films, artists create computer **graphics** of anything from giant waves to armies of aliens and then add them to a real film. Some CGI characters look almost as realistic as real actors!

This may look like a real actor, but it is actually a CGI effect.

CAPTURING MOVEMENTS

How do film artists make **CGI** characters have life-like expressions and move around realistically? They use motion capture. This is when film makers create special film of how parts of an actor's body change position when it moves. A computer program uses the film to create a moving skeleton on-screen. Artists then draw flesh and clothing onto the skeleton to make it look real.

The markers studded all over the actor Tom Hanks change position as he moves.

Seeing dots

For motion capture an actor usually puts on a special suit and hat covered with little lights called markers. Many of the markers are positioned at joints, such as the knees, where the skeleton moves. The **film crew** also stick markers on the actor's face. These markers pick up facial expressions. Then camera operators record film of the markers using movie cameras.

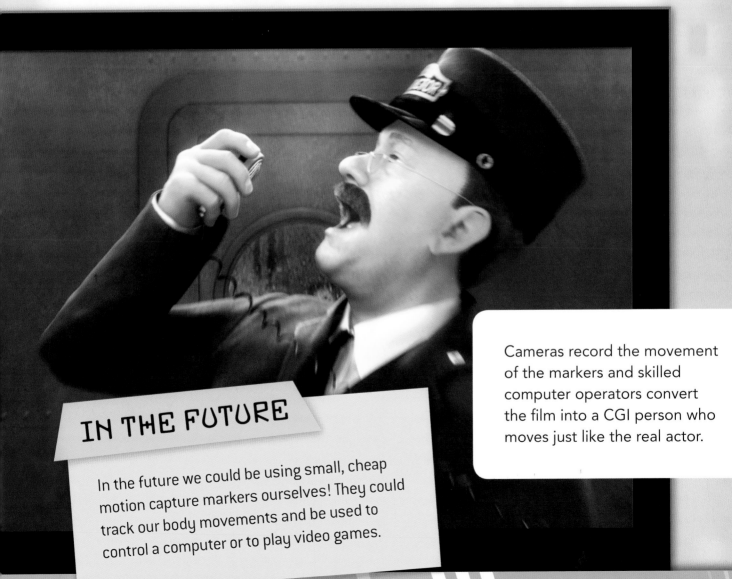

Cameras record the movement of the markers and skilled computer operators convert the film into a CGI person who moves just like the real actor.

IN THE FUTURE

In the future we could be using small, cheap motion capture markers ourselves! They could track our body movements and be used to control a computer or to play video games.

SOUND

Films need sound — a whispering voice, echoing footsteps, or gentle music all help to create the right mood. Voices and other sounds are captured by **microphones** on a film set. These **machines** convert sound into electrical messages or signals. Some microphones are small and hidden inside an actor's clothes. Others are bigger and hang above the actors from a long pole called a boom.

A boom holds the microphone close to the speaking actors without appearing in the film.

Sound effects

Some sounds are recorded and added to a film after it has been finished. Composers are people who write music especially to go with the mood of the film. Workers called foley artists provide film sound effects. They store recordings of many sound effects, such as vehicle engine noises or background chatter. They create others using various objects.

Foley artists might shake vines or walk on sand to create realistic sounds for the film.

AT WORK

MAKING NOISES

Foley artists invent ways of making sounds for films. The sound of walking in crunchy snow can be made by treading in salt and corn starch, and the sound of a horse walking on a road can be made by knocking coconut shells together!

INSIDE A MICROPHONE

Sound happens when something **vibrates** or shakes quickly. Vibrating objects make the air around them move in **sound waves**. Sound waves move out from vibrations a bit like ripples after you drop a stone in a pond. Our ears convert sound waves into signals that our brain recognizes as sounds.

Microphones are very important for film actors. The illustration on page 25 shows how they work.

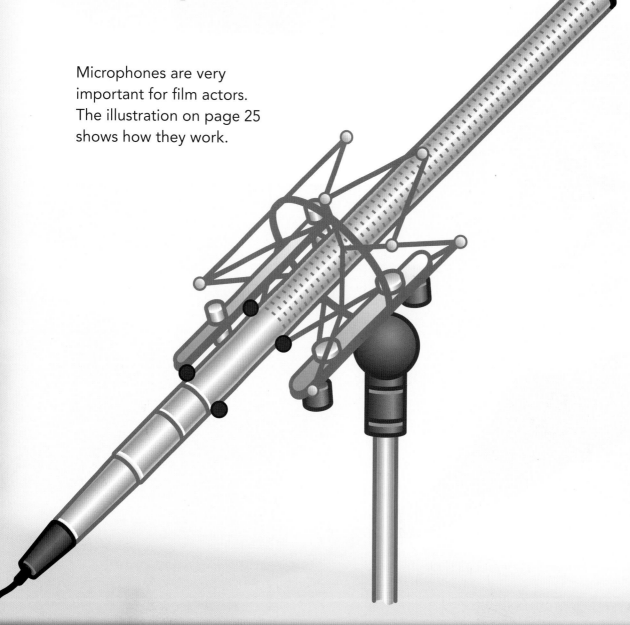

The magnet makes an electric current move through the vibrating coil and into the wires to the amplifier.

Springs make the diaphragm bounce back after each sound wave.

Dust cover

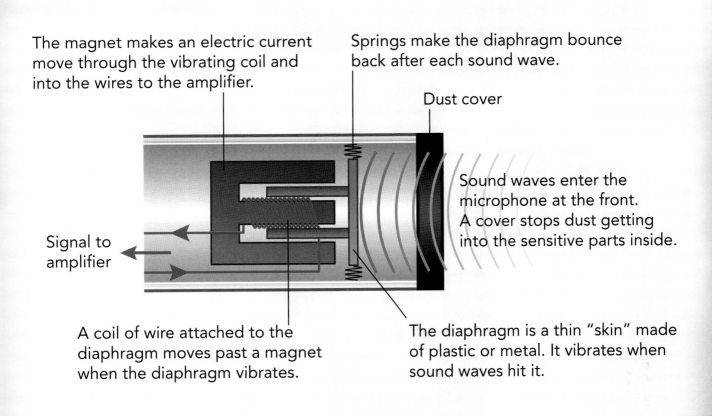

Signal to amplifier

Sound waves enter the microphone at the front. A cover stops dust getting into the sensitive parts inside.

A coil of wire attached to the diaphragm moves past a magnet when the diaphragm vibrates.

The diaphragm is a thin "skin" made of plastic or metal. It vibrates when sound waves hit it.

Microphones convert sound waves into tiny electrical signals. Sound production mixers use **machines** called **amplifiers** to make the signals bigger. They then record the signals onto computers. When we watch a film, the recorded signals are converted back into sound waves using machines called **loudspeakers**.

SHOWING THE FILM

At the cinema we watch films on a large, wide screen. The **machine** that plays the film is called a **projector**. The projector makes images bigger and shines them on flat surfaces. In some cinemas the projectors have **motors** that move strips of film past a bright light. The light shines through each transparent image of the film. A **lens** magnifies (enlarges) the image onto the screen.

3D films

Some projectors make actors seem to leap out of the screen! These machines show two slightly different versions of the same film at the same time. The audience wears special glasses to make the film images merge together. Then the film seems to be **three-dimensional** (3D).

AT WORK

IMAX CINEMAS

Sometimes IMAX cinemas show 3D films on giant screens that curve halfway around the room. This makes the audience feel as if they are really inside the film. Some IMAX screens are huge. The screen at the IMAX cinema in London is as tall as five double-decker buses stacked on top of each other!

3D cinemas like this one have seats that shake or tilt during films, so the audience really feels like they are part of the action!

FILM TECHNOLOGY

In the dark of a cinema we are surrounded by the action and sounds of a film. The **projector** and the **loudspeakers** in a cinema play images and sounds created in a film studio by cameras and **microphones**. But the quality of film these pieces of technology produce depends on many other things, from lighting and sound, to special effects and bluescreens.

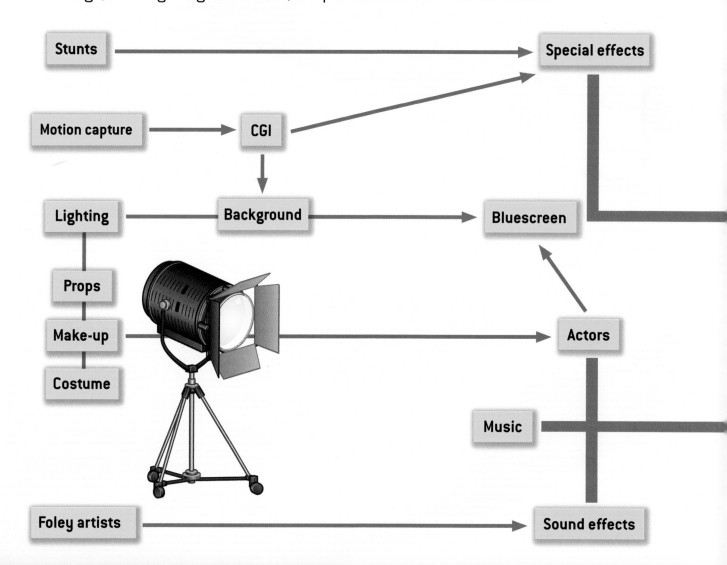

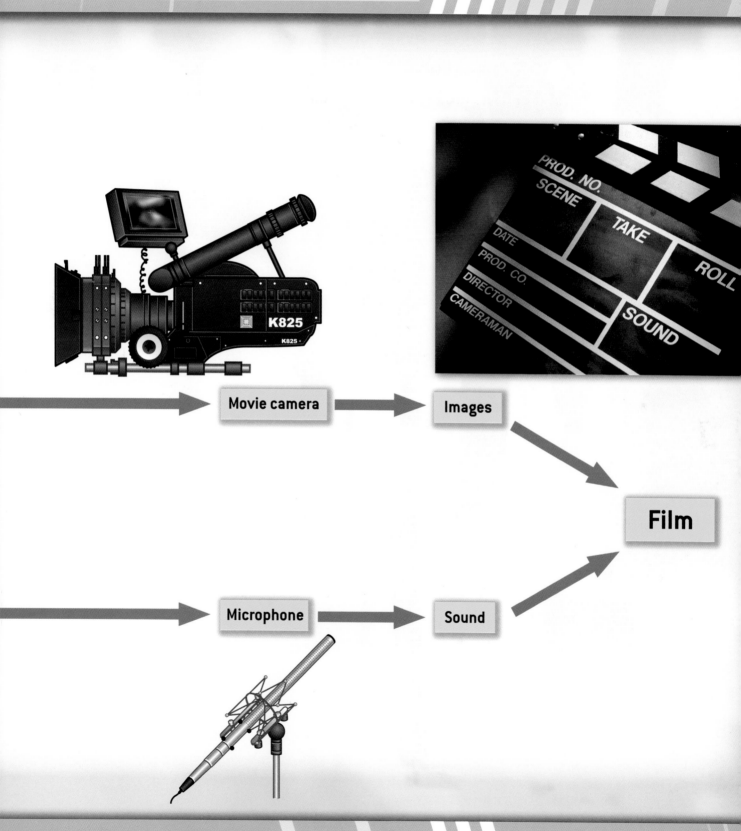

Movie camera → Images

Microphone → Sound

Images → Film ← Sound

K825

PROD. NO.
SCENE
DATE
PROD. CO.
DIRECTOR
CAMERAMAN
TAKE
ROLL
SOUND

GLOSSARY

amplifier device used to increase the power of an electronic signal. In a sound system the amplifier is what makes noises louder.

cast shape that forms from a mould. When you remove jelly from a mould it is a kind of cast. (Cast is also a word for the group of actors in a film.)

CGI computer generated images. *Toy Story* (1995) was the first full-length CGI film.

computer chip tiny piece of electronic equipment. Computer chips control functions of some machines.

energy energy makes things work

film crew group of people that work together to make a film

filter device that removes something from whatever passes through it. A net curtain is a kind of filter, because it only lets a certain amount of light through.

graphic image that is generated by a computer. Computer graphics are used in many films today.

lens the part of a camera that concentrates light and focuses the image

location place where a film is made. A location for a cowboy film can be a desert.

loudspeaker device that converts electrical signals into sounds

machine device that helps us do work

microphone device that changes sounds into electric signals

motor machine that converts electrical energy into rotating or turning energy

mould container into which liquid is poured to create a shape. When the liquid hardens in the mould it forms that shape.

projector machine that enables images and films to be displayed on a screen

prop item an actor touches or uses on the set of a movie or play. A prop could be a book, a table, or a tennis racket.

sensor device that senses light or other signals and produces an electronic signal from them

sound wave invisible wave in the air

special effect effect used to produce scenes that cannot be achieved by normal techniques. Special effects include spaceships and exploding buildings.

spotlight light that shines down on a stage or film set

stunt difficult or dangerous trick. In films stunts are usually performed by specially trained people, not by actors.

three-dimensional something with height, width, and depth. In 3D cinemas images look as if you could walk around them!

vibrate move back and forth rapidly

FIND OUT MORE

Books

Backstage at a Movie Set, Katherine Wessling (Children's Press, 2003)

Filming a Blockbuster (Behind the Scenes), Peter Mellett (Heinemann Library, 2000)

Lights, Camera, Action!: Making Movies and TV from the Inside Out, Lisa O'Brien (Maple Tree Press, 2007)

Movie Makeup, Costumes, and Sets (Making Movies), Geoffrey M. Horn (Gareth Stevens Publishing, 2006)

Websites

www.filmstreet.co.uk

Here you can find tips for making your own films.

www.moxie.com

Create your own moving picture flipbooks.

www.pixar.com/howwedoit

Discover some of the secrets behind how Pixar made amazing animations like *Toy Story*.

www.zuzu.org/printout.html

Learn about animation by making your own flip book and printing it out.

INDEX